THE POETRY OF EVERYTHING

By R.e Taylor

Shadowlight Publishing
Redbank Plains, Queensland, Australia

www.shadowlightbooks.com

ISBN # 978-0-9942128-6-3

Dedication

I do hereby, by the power invested to me by the
universe, dedicate this book of poetry
to everything, everybody and every place
in our ever expanding universe which inspires
poets, artists, songwriters, authors and actors to
create such beauty in the world.

Okay, now with the legalese stuff that I have to say.

© 2016 Shadowlight Publishing

I have to tell you that you may NOT steal, borrow, or reproduce anything from this book. Everything is protected by international copyright. If you want to use it… to write to Shadowlight Publishing and ask. We will most likely say okay, but you do have to ask first!

The Poetry of Everything

Everything has a poem hidden inside
Feelings that the world does not know
Stories that will never be told
Words that may never be read
We poets look beyond the surface
To find the words hidden deep inside
We listen to what everything has to say
We share it all with the world
And through us everything has a voice

Teddy Bear

It is so sad to see a teddy bear
Left all alone
Where is the child you loved
The one you comforted during the storms
The one who told you all their secrets
The one who promised
They would always be your friend
The one you protected
From the monsters under the bed
You know they didn't mean to leave you
Drop you in a place where you may never be found
You know that they loved you too much for that
They have more secrets to share
There will be a million more storms
There will always be a monster under the bed
In that child's mind
When they are frightened, they will think of you
Remember that you were there for them
Remember that you kept them safe
And if you are lucky another child will find you
Take you home and share their secrets with you
Hide under the blankets with you in a storm
And show you the monsters
Monsters who hide under their bed
Then, maybe they will make you their bestest friend

The Fires of Love

Smoke floats into the air
Coming from a heart that burns for you
Ignited when I first looked into your eyes
Stoked when we shared our first kiss
Even when the flames faded to embers
When words were spoken in anger
They grew again when my hand touched yours
They are all consuming
Burning my heart, my mind and my soul
The flames cannot be controlled
Nor should they ever be
Long after my body has gone from this world
The fires will burn far into the next world

The Beauty of the Falling Rain

There is a beauty in the falling
The ringing sound as it hits a copper roof
Performing nature's symphony
The sheets of water roll down a glass window
Distorting the reality outside
Or maybe it makes it more real
Imagination flourishes in the warped images
Images that bring on new feelings
Feelings of warmth and love
As it cleanses the world around it
The mind travels through this new world
Fantasies of distant forests
Lands of lush greens
Richer than any ever seen by man
Fields of waving grass
A dance that started millennia ago
A dance still performed by a young girl
Dressed in a white flowing dress
She dances in clothes soaked to the bones
The blue halo of rain around a distant light surrounds her
As she hears the music of the rain on the street
She looks to the heavens
To the dark clouds above her
She thanks them for every drop of rain
And she prays for the next downpour
When she can dance again

Imagination

Somewhere there is a world
A place where anything can happen
There can be wars and peace where everyone lives
Animals long extinct roaming with modern man
Islands with only one inhabitant
Foods with flavors never tasted before
Kisses that never end from women who don't exist
And couples who never argue
Clean air and always sunny skies
And never, ever a flake of snow
Such a world is only in my mind

Not in a dream
It is somewhere every person has within them
A magical land called imagination
Where everyone can see what they want to see
Where they can be who they want to be
All you have to do is open the door
And you will be welcome

One Tree

You came across the water
Taking land that did not belong to you
You chased the natives from their homes
Killing some for no reason
Locking some away in dark cells
You put the rest on compounds
Places where you could control them
Then you hunted the animals
So many we are down to the last few
They were both here long before you
Man and animal settled this land
While you and yours lived in caves
Now the land is yours
My home has been taken from me
So I, like so many wander the land
Looking for a chance to live in peace
Now, I have only one question
Asking for an answer just for me

In your haste to kill and control this land
Couldn't you just leave one tree standing
One tree where I could sleep, eat and live
I guess not

The Unwritten History of The Prairie Wind

Rotten timbers lay deep in a field
Remnants of a cabin built years ago
Built by pioneers from the East
A family looking for a new world
Free of the city's constraints
They thrived with fields of wheat
Waving in the mild prairie breeze
Miles from the nearest neighbor
They lived peacefully
Away from the problems they knew
In their previous lives
Now the air was sweet and clear
The songs of birds floated around the cabin
Children played in the grasses
Now they are all gone
Lost to an unwritten history
Was it a war, a plague, and Indian attack?
Are the buried beneath the fertile land?
Or did they just leave?
No one knows except the grass and it won't tell
The rotted timbers will never tell
They just remember
The family
The children
The hopes of a pioneer
All lost to the prairie winds.

Let The Light Shine

Let the light shine
Cutting through our lives
Showing that there is hope
Despite what you see
What you hear
Or what you know
Somewhere the light is shining
Showing people how to live
How to change to end the darkness
What need to be done to survive
The light will become brighter
More intense as people learn
As people accept differences
Thinking they don't understand
Losing hatred raised from ignorance
Let them all know the truth
The light will shine
Knowledge will grow
And life will be better
If we let the light shine

Photo courtesy Elizabeth Waterhouse

The Girl I Used To Know

I know what I wanted to say
The words were there
My mind thought out just what to say
They have been there so long
But, when I see you they disappear
Other thoughts take their place
Memories of you from long ago
When you were in my arms
When my eyes looked into your heart
And I saw you for who you really were
Tee shirts, ponytails and thick framed glasses

You are no longer the woman I kissed
The one who owned my heart and soul
Over the years you changed
Your face and hair became too beautiful
Your body became a statue of a goddess
Flawless, perfect beyond belief
You chose diamonds and designer gowns
Your choices ruined the girl you used to be
You became too good for a poor country boy
A boy from the wrong side of the street
But you know that this boy never changed
I still remember and dream of you
However, I will keep my words
Hidden deep inside me
For now, I will just look at you and remember
When you were just the girl I knew a long time ago

Hope

The world is crumbling around you
Everything you knew is gone
Your mummy and daddy
In graves a city away
Taken from you for no reason
Other than the anger of others
Hang on little one
There are lights in your future
You can see them in your eyes
In the eyes of the puppy you hold
Someday the anger will end
Your world will again be happy
But for now love your puppy

Hold it tight to your chest
Treasure it as you would your life
It will always be there for you
Filled with the love you lost
My dream is that you name it Hope
Because that is what you need right now
You need to hold onto hope
As long as you can

A Poet's Thoughts

I am luckier than most
I have a special place to write
A small room
No larger than a bathroom
It is neither a palace nor a ghetto
It is just a place where
I can be alone with my thoughts
I know it has been used by artists before
An old pine-wood table bears the name Picasso
Etched into the top so deep and so many years ago
Canvases and papers cover the walls
Unfinished pieces
From a dozen generations of creativity
I wonder why they were never finished
It is a thought I could never answer
I know the words come to me
My pen scribes them to sheets of yellowing paper
They may never sell
No one may ever have the chance to read them
I may never include them in a book
But they are my words
My thoughts and my yellowing paper
No one can ever take that away from me
It is just me alone in my room
And that is how I want it

A Bluish Violet Flower

A bluish violet flower watches
From the shore of an ancient riverbed
A river born of fire when the Earth was new
Sulfuric air, ground ripped apart
From Earth's upheaval
Chemicals mixed with lightening to create life
Single-celled animals and ancient reptiles
And a single plant on the burnt earth
A single plant with a single bluish violet flower
It lived its life with cooling water
Cattails lined the shore
A million flowers bloomed every spring
Fish and turtles swam in its currents
Children played on its shore
Laughing and jumping into the refreshing waters

The waters caressed the bluish violet flower
Giving it lifesaving moisture
Still the bluish violet flower, watched the fish,
The turtles and the children
The river long ago died
The riverbed that, from the beginning held life
Is still now
Rocks of sandstones and granite
Create a natural blanket
The only fish are fossils of life millions of years old
That bluish violet flower
The one whose life began when time was young
The one who watched when life began and thrived in a lonely riverbed
It remembers the fish, the turtles
The children and the flowers
That bluish violet flower still watches
It watches the stillness and the silence
And all alone, it mourns

My Last Fairy

Mom and dad
Why did you tell me the truth
I was so young
Just a little child
Full of hope and faith
I believed in Santa Clause
The Easter Bunny and fairies
They were alive for me
You didn't have to tell me
I didn't want to know
Santa Clause is just a man in a suit
The Easter Bunny isn't real
The fairies had been just the stuff of stories
You didn't watch as my youth died that day

You didn't see me cry when I went to bed
You never told me
That would be the night my last fairy friend died
If only I would not have listened
If I would have followed my heart
That fairy would have been flying around my room
And maybe I would still believe in miracles

A Gift From The Gods

Storm clouds over distant hills
Flashes of light as lightning strikes the Earth
Blue skies above give hope
Gentle breezes cover the sound of thunder
You know the rain will come
Be sure the winds will blow
The rain has to come
The wind has to come
For now, enjoy the momentary sun
Just know that it is a gift from the gods
To be lived and loved

Beauty

Do you know that you are beautiful
Has anyone told you so
Your body is not a size 3
Nor should it be
You are the perfect you
Diets and fads would ruin who you are
Your smile reflects your beauty
Your eyes show the fantastic soul you have
Do not pay attention to the ads
Do not compare yourself to a starving model
You are not what ignorant people see
You are the woman you should be
You are beautiful

A Child's Smile

A thousand pieces of cloth
A dozen different colors
A hundred different designs
Each shaped to fit
Cut by hand
Pieced together
Edges close enough to become one
Stitch by stitch
Following centuries-old traditions
A complex pattern is revealed
The quilt grows before the artist's eyes
After a week she makes the last stitch
The piece now has a life of its own
That night she sees her quilt one more time
It covers a little girl

No more than three years old
Protecting her from the cold of winter
The child smiles as she pulls it close
And a tear rolls down the quilter's cheek
Her work is done
Her only payment was the child's smile
And that was all she ever wanted.

The Goddess

How could anyone ever meet you
Such a beauty to behold
Are you an angel from Heaven
A queen from a lost time
A goddess who fell to Earth
Your eyes do show your soul
Just enough to tease anyone who looks at you
But not enough for anyone to know you
All we have is your beauty
The mystery in your face
Please give us a chance to meet you

Your heart and your soul
Give us a chance to see the real you
So we can get to know you
And have a chance to love you

My '67 VW

I remember the moment I saw you
Sitting in the sun
I fell in love and swept you away
We travelled the world together
Places I never thought I'd ever see
We went to see Woodstock
Rockets launch from Cape Kennedy
You were there when I met my first love
And my second and third
My kids played with you in the front yard
Took you on road trips to God knows where
And even learned about life with you by their side
But all good things leave
It is just part of nature
You were in my life for so long
My good times and, the times I wanted to die
You were there.
The night you died
I sat with a shot glass in my hand
A half empty bottle of Jack resting in my lap
And I cried

Aboriginal Sweet Water

This land has always been my home
More than two thousand generations
My people have shared this land
Living their lives and all they offered
Songs and stories filled the air
That was long ago when then sweet water flowed
Feeding the land and keeping us alive
Emus lay their eggs in plentiful nests
Roos ran wild in our bush
They fed our babies and gave us clothes
And we were a proud people
And the sweet water came at night
The water is now gone
Evaporated by the desert sun
The Roos and Emus have moved on
Nature and Australia have turned their backs on us
Our traditions are still among us
We are still a proud people
We can and will survive no matter what
The spirits will hear our prayers
They will grant our wishes
The sweet water will once again flow
We will once again be in paradise
And our songs can once again be heard

Sweet & Innocent

You look so innocent
Sweet and charming as can be
Yet, your eyes show the truth
Your face shows the real you
I know you are planning something
It could be throwing your food
Pulling the dog by the ears
Or sneaking out of your nap
I know you are planning something
It's there in your evil little smile
Still, when you do what you're going to do
Whether it be the food, the dog or the nap
I will always love you
I will always care for you
But... I never said I wouldn't get even

The Unknown Poet

A poem written ages ago
Written but unsigned
Who was the poet?
He hid his identity for history
Why did he write such terrible words?
What was in his mind?
Were they his dreams?
Did he live in such pain?
Reading and rereading his words
You can see into his soul
If only we knew his name

Moonflower

The sun is long since gone
The last strains of its light
Faded behind the horizon
The moon shines down on a sleeping world
Stars twinkle with their own beautiful light
Animals move on their nightly paths
Birds make lonely calls looking for a single friend
On the ground the moon flower opens
Catching every bit of light, it shows its beauty
No one will get the chance to see it bloom
The coming of the sun hides
What only the night brings
Such beauty wasted in the night

The Good Old Days

Thinking back to the beginnings of my life
Two wars, America could never have won
Thousands dead, more wounded, as America fought
A president murdered
As he waved at the people who loved him
Riots that placed whites against blacks
Broke out in every city
Four innocents killed for speaking their mind
Others jailed and beaten for protesting
A president they thought was wrong
Free speech was only for the party in power
A wall built to separate families
From ever seeing each, other mocked American power
Nuclear war was less than ninety miles away
While the president flexed his muscle
American missiles were stationed all across the country
So we could destroy any enemy
Strikes lasted not weeks, but months
Causing people to live in their cars
No one came to help as children starved
The president committed crimes
Yet, was never punished
What was a crime, was erased by his friend
Stating the president would be pardoned
That ended that
People talk about the good old days
Look at history and let me know when they were
Then we can talk about the good old days
And where they were hiding

Just The Right Words

Where are the words I imagined last night?
They were so clear and strong
Saying exactly, what I wanted to say
I knew what they were
I had them memorized
They kept me awake until I got them just right
But how could I tell them
My mouth isn't worthy to say them
My hands are not talented enough to write them
My heart is barely strong enough to feel what they convey
Those words are said way too often
They are words that don't say enough
Maybe if I whispered them
Barely above a breath
They would mean something
You would hear them and smile
Only then I would know
That they were the right words all along

Hidden By A Blue Sky

Sky
Light blue
Eternal
Mixing colors
A prism united
Hiding endless darkness
Worlds orbiting distant stars
Innumerable living planets
Will they be intelligent like us?
Does their blue sky allow them to know us?

Where Did The Memories Go?

Where did all the memories go?
The stories we were told as kids
Ignored as the ramblings of the old
Stories not connected with our time
Not happening in our space
Not part of our lives
Why should they matter?
Horror and starvation
The disease that took the lives of millions
War in distant lands, killing sons and brothers
Atrocities done for many reasons
All beyond a man's imagination
Yet they survived the pain
They remember through tortured dreams
Through tears flow down a rutted cheek
From vacant eyes that stare into space
All they wish is for someone to listen
Maybe not believe… just listen
Is that too much to ask
After all they went through to survive
To live long enough to share their story with us
Where did all the memories go?
Ignored as the ramblings of the old
Lost because of the ignorance of the young
Stories never again to be told
Yet, destined to be repeated

Something To Be Learned

Were those eyes yours
They looked across the trees of a virgin forest
Water as clear as a brisk winter sky
The sand brushed by wind blowing off the ancient sea
People, you see people
Children of nature
Worship the spirits all around them
Never harming nature
Leaving only footprints wherever they travel
Alone for a thousand year they look at you
Watching, seeing what you may do
You watch back

Curious, afraid
You do not understand
How can people live like this
You desire what they have
You see the smiles in their faces
The joy of their children
The way they live
How their spirits protect them
You wish as you watch
You want to be like them
But what they have, you will never share
You do not understand
For you a rock is a rock
A tree is a tree
These people see differently
Everything is vital
Everything is alive
Everything has a soul
That is something you have not learned yet
You desire what they have
You want to be like them
When will you stop listening to your mind
When will you listen with your heart
You have a lifetime to learn
The desire is not there
Let your mind and heart become one
Accept them
Learn from them
Take the time you need
Then smile, accept them as brothers
And you will become one with the spirits

In Your Eyes

Looking in your eyes
There is everything I need to see
A lifetime of pain
Moments of pleasure
I see your thoughts
Your soul
Your dreams
Without a word
I know how you feel
The love in your heart
Flows through your eyes of the deepest blue
Your eyes stare
Looking at me
Looking into my eyes
Into my soul
Into my heart
Hoping that you see what I see
I will never say a word

A whisper will not pass my lips
Words cannot share our feelings
They will only detract
Take away from the honesties
My eyes
Your eyes
Say it alone
It is all in our eyes

The Little Blue Flower

I looked out my window
On the grass I had mowed dozens of times
In the dimness between two houses
You were there, newly born
The fleeting light shone on your petals
Blue as a baby's eyes
The same look of innocence
The same illusion of purity
Their white edges reflected the golden morning light
They were as small as a second and begging to be noticed
I watched you reach for the sky
Through the light snow that fell during the night
I had to leave but your image played through my head.
Your beauty in a world of coldness
The way you stood when all the others had fallen
When I returned I saw that you had gone
Did I dream you?
Were you never there in the first place?

Looking through the window I see a little girl
She was maybe five years of age
Her red hair tied on top of her head
A small pink ribbon blows softly in the breeze
There you are... riding with her... making her smile
Young and innocent
Pretty and sweet
I see that the two of you belong together
I cry, tears flow down my cheeks
Not at my loss
But rather at the joy that little girl has found.

Summertime Fog

I know there is a sun above
The stars have long since faded away
Fog has turned the world a dark blue
The morning dew still clings beneath my feet
A chill pierces through my jacket
Although it is a June morning
It feels like November
Thoughts rush through my head
Dreams of a Winter
Visions of the beach I left behind
That girl in the pink bikini sitting in the sun
Fishing in a pond, so warm
So desirable to this
Distant and oh so far away
Will I ever see it again
When this mist clears… it is so cold
Animal tracks break up the pearls of water
Leaving a path to follow
One beam of sun
A single beam of light
Hope, far away yet there
Leading me out of the darkness
Into a world of light and warmth
Back to the fishing hole
Back to the beach
And to that girl
Sitting there in her pink bikini

The Heart Rules
As The Mind Wanders

What does it mean?
I look at you and feel love
But I do not know if it is you I love
Or the dream of you
I think about you all of the time
The feel of your skin
The smell of your hair
The way your eyes sparkle
As you look at a Summer's full moon
You take me back
I was younger and did not know
What love was
How could I tell
What should I look for?
Are there words I should hear?
A lifetime older now
Thoughts swim in oceans of confusion
Not knowing is killing me
My heart tells me what to do
What to say
What to feel
My mind wanders
Slow and confused
My heart rules and I fall in love

Mother Nature's Mistake

Hills that go on for miles
Pines, oaks and maples, reach for the sky
Their leafs casting a cooling shade on a hot summer day
Animals of all kinds dance in the gentle breeze
Flowers fill in the green blanket of meadow grass
Added beauty from a gracious Mother Nature
You sat among this beauty
Glowing in the late evening's golden sun
Mother Nature watches as her work fades
She sees you and knows that she cannot match your beauty
So she created the night to try and hide you
But your beauty cannot be hidden
You were made to be beautiful
That was Mother Nature's one mistake
She created one being more beautiful
Than anything she could ever create again
And for that she should be praised
And thanked for giving you to the world

The Old Man In The Mirror

Who is that old man who looks at me in the morning?
When I shave and showed
He is there living in a pane of glass
Grey hairs replacing the dark walnut brown
More and more each day, each hour
Eyes looking tired from ages of struggles
Each reflecting a soul which was once so full of life
Now it lays stagnant and lost
It has the memories of its youth
Doing things that man can now only remember
Wrinkles took so long to show
Even fooling that old man
Into thinking he was younger than he is
Every grey hair, every wrinkle has been earned
They are the wages of pain and anxiety of aging
Some called them badges of honor
I look in the mirror
And see that old man looking back at me
I don't see honor, pain, stress or anxiety
That old man looking back at me has lived a full life
Successes and mistakes of the past
Are reflected in the mirror
Lost loves and loves found are hidden in his spirit
I look at the old man in the mirror
I look at the grey hair and the sad eyes
I see each and every wrinkle
I look at the old man in the mirror, and I see life

The Garden

Roses and violets grow wild, yet tamed in raised gardens
English boxwood and laurel line the white gravel footpath
Butterflies and bees float
And buzz around a thousand flowers
Their sounds melding with the footsteps of visitors
Walking through this world
Every sense is awakened and teased
But, could the mind take in all the sights
Smells and sounds surrounding it?
The smell of mint wafting through the breezes
Is easy to notice
However, the mild sweetness of the zinnia
And snapdragons will not be ignored
The sounds of a fountain echo off distant walls
Walls that have held generations of grape vines and ivy
Hummingbirds dart wildly around
Looking for their favorite nectar
Other birds just sit on the walls
And watch what is happening
Life stays the same within the isolated ecosystem
Days, weeks, months, years, or decades
None of it matters
It is Nature's canvas to do with as she wishes
Her canvas, her palette, her paint and her brushes
That garden is her artwork to enjoy
And wonder at for all time

The Quilter

A hundred pieces of cloth
Each a different pattern and color
Diamonds, squares and triangles
Each measured by the eyes of an artist
Each cut one by one with a steady hand
Small pieces with no identity
Sewn together hour after hour
Their beauty comes from unique patterns
Patterns passed down through ages of artists
Each one, when it is finished tells a story
A piece of history in every stitch
Every seam, an artist's vision in itself
There is a moment of pleasure
When the last stitch is made
Pride in a piece of creation
In that moment a spark fills the artist
A spark that cannot be quenched no matter what
Another hundred pieces of cloth come out of hiding
And another quilt is started

The Girl In The Window

How could anyone ever forget?
Such beautiful paintings
Each hung carefully
Lit with just the right light
People walk by day after day
They look but they are not looking
They see such a memorable picture
A city at its glory
Berlin in the beginning of the Third Reich
A thousand red flags with black broken crosses
People wearing colorful clothes
Each with a smile on their faces
A paradise on planet Earth
They look but they are not looking
They do not see right in front of them
Hiding in a window is a young girl
A girl of no more than nine years old
Such pain and torture can be seen as she reaches for help
There is a tiny six-pointed yellow star on her chest
Even sixty five years later no one sees her
No one sees the secret the artist put in his world
Could people be so blind to someone in need?
Did that little girl live?
Was she tortured and killed alone in a prison camp
Her story was never told
But she did more that even the toughest soldier
Her face, the tears flowing down her cheeks
She cried for help for six million people
It was all there to see
If only anyone had taken the time to look

God Gave Us Bacon

God gave man a gift
Something special for a cold morning
Something we have eaten for centuries
We grew up on it
We learned to love it
We learned that we cannot live without it
Spiced and smoked
It is something we desire
Sometimes more than our friends
Sometimes more than our families
We need it with lettuce and tomato
Fried eggs and toasts
Even on our grilled hamburgers
Some say that God's gift will kill us
How can that be so
Bacon was a treat given to man
It was made to complete our lives
To the neigh sayers who bad mouth our food
Think of this when you speak such things
Without bacon what would we do with all the pigs
And what would make our eating so much fun
So join with the rest of us
Open your mouth and cheer the all mighty bacon
After all, it will be here long after you are gone
And we will celebrate with a BLT
And just maybe a nice cold beer
And we won't save you one

Country Girl

Worn Levi's sitting on a torn seat
Leather boots pushing down on the pedals
She grips tightly on a Harley shifter
Jumping from third to fifth and back again
Her pickup truck tears down the country road
Leaving a cloud of dust where ever she goes
She's a girl of the backwoods
Wild and living free
She is the fantasy every country boy has
The woman no city boy can touch
She is a country girl
Born listening to Hank Jr.
She still says Mama and y'all
Y'all, got to love a country girl
She is truly one of a kind

Outback Sunset

Sitting under an old gum tree
The one down by the creek
Miles away from the road
My truck got me there
Just as if it had a heart of its own
The girl I love at my side
And a Mason Jar full of Aussie moonshine in my hand
Fog rolls in over the outback
As the sun turns from white to a deep red
I am so happy to be here to experience it
To live to see the truest beauty of Heaven
Paradise couldn't be any better than an Outback sunset

Mud of the Mind

Thousands of years of mud
Wrapped around my legs
Struggling to reach my mind
To force me to see a reality, I didn't create
Others decided what I should see
What I should hear
And what I should believe
I want to be free of their mud
The ideas they approve of
The thoughts they want me to have
I do not believe their visions
That Cinderella was a good girl
The Wicked Witch was evil
They may have been right
They may have been wrong
Once the mud they created is gone
My mind will tell me the truth
And I will see a reality
Maybe one they cannot accept
But for me it will be true
And that will be all that matters

Test Pattern

Such memories
Lost long ago
In an innocent time
Before computers
Before cell phone
And video games
Kids stayed awake
Hours after going to bed
Hiding under our blankets
Waiting for our parents to go to bed
When we snuck downstairs
Turned on our old B&W TV
Watching until Jack Paar finished
Until the Star-Spangled Banner played
Long before the daily crop reports
The station shut down until morning
Then we were able to see it
Our friend, the test pattern
Circles and targets
Different shades from black to white
And that Indian chief
Seeing him told us it was time to get to bed
To sleep until morning
So we could watch Captain Kangaroo
And be kids

The Bridge

I know that you are there
Somewhere in the mist
Hidden by time
Existing only in fading memories
There is a path back to you
A bridge, that I may not cross
So I stand and look
Wanting so badly to cross
Enter the mist of time
So I can try to find you
And my memories will become real
If only I can cross the bridge

The Wise Old Tree

Wise Old Tree
What have you seen
What have you learned over the years
Did you see the first person to walk this land
The sadness of all those who died in wars
Who was the first to look at you in the sunset
How many couples fell in love beneath your boughs
Began their lives together
Shared gold bands with you and God as their witness
Did children tell stories of the creatures in your branches
Did they run when the wind rustled your leaves
Wise Old Tree
You have such a glorious history
A life all except you can only dream of
You are immortal
A god hiding in the forest
Keep your stories
Your secrets
Until you feel we are ready
Then we will listen and learn
And we will be better for it

The Loss of Dragons

Why did you disappear
You were the stuff of legends
Making kings and heroes
The small towns were afraid of you
They hid their children
Ran to the forests to hide
Still, they sang songs about you
Told stories that are still told today
Then you were just gone
New stories were no longer written
Songs never again sang of you
New demons frightened the people
New legends made kings and heroes

Even now, without the songs and stories
The people need you
You stand in bronze and granite
Guarding our churches and buildings
We look at you in amazement
Impressed by your wings and fangs
Still, there are no new legends or songs
No more kings and heroes
And that is sad

Missing Out On Beauty

I cannot help you
As much as I want to
You're in a world
Where beauty doesn't exist
You cannot look at a flower
Read a poem
Or look at a painting
Money is your life
The only thing you love
More than your heart
More than your family
More than what you should feel
Have you seen your daughter's drawing
The one on the fridge
She made it for you
But you were too busy to see it
Have you heard the poem from the boy next door
He put his whole heart into it
But you won't listen
Some things are more important
They will make you smile
Brighten your heart and soul
Take the time to look and listen
See what the world has to offer
The money will still be there
But someday your daughter will not draw
The poet will no longer write
That will be a day part of the world dies
And you will not notice

Mother Earth

Listen to the beating heart of our world
Feel as she stretches and changes
Her breath as it blows through your hair
We have abused her
Taken everything she has to offer
Hurt her in ways that she never deserved
Even though we are mere parasites
Germs infecting her skin
Still, she holds us and cherishes us
As any mother would her children
However, until now we haven't cared
She gave and gave without asking for anything
She does not need us to save her
Despite it all, she is strong
After the scars we inflicted have faded
The wounds have all healed
Our mother will heal herself
She will bring back the life she once had
She will forgive us
This time

In The World Between Sleep And Reality

I lay in my bed
Blankets wrapped around my ankles
My mind wondered why should I awaken
I was living in that world between sleep and reality
My mind takes me places I always wanted to see
Lands lost to time
Brightly lit cities millions of miles away
I meet people who I never would have met
If I were in the real world
People of legends
Told of long lost ancient tongues
They sit with me and we talk about the meaning of life
Sharing their wisdom in marble temples
Looking around it is an entire world
There are valleys lush with tropical plants
Their skies filled with deep green leaves
Birds of red, blue, violet and yellow
Fill the air with a symphony of sounds
Notes melding into a perfection of music
Mountains, blue and snow-capped

Unexplored and never seen
I can see women whose beauty is beyond compare
Share a drink with me in dark taverns
They tell me about their feelings
And, occasionally they give me a kiss
It is a world that I know well
It is a place where I am accepted for who I am
Then I awake
The lands, the music and the women
Fade into the morning light
My eyes focus
My mind sharpens
The real world invades my thoughts
But I remember that when the sun sets
My eyes will close and once again
I will be in a world of my own creation
And I, tomorrow morning
I know I will not want to awake
And I will ask, why can't I stay asleep

Let Me Read To You

Let me read to you
Tell you the stories my mother told me
Hear the words I read
Let your mind wander
Seeing the world of fairies and angels
Princesses and heroes
Learn that love really exists
The hope is in everything
Let me read to you as you fall asleep
So you may dream of happiness
And the nightmares will be kept away
Let me read to you
Because I love you and I want you to be happy
So that you may write your own fairy tales
And you will read them to your children
So, let me read to you

What Does A Poet See

What does a poet see?
It is a consciousness some lack?
Is that how we see beauty in everything?
The hidden world inside a blooming flower
So many colors in a sunset
Even the reflective surface in an ice cube
Our minds see so much that many do not see
Our words describe the reality we see
A reality we created as our own
Our pens are the paint brushes of the gods
We share feelings, no one will talk about
If they realize that they even exist
What does a poet see?
We see beauty and hope in everything
If not for the lowly poet
How would the world know that beauty exists?

A Green Dog Loves Decent Purple Dandelions

I knew I had it with me
It gave me so many great ideas
Shaped them and formed them into poetry
Lately the words do not come to me
They mix together and become incomprehensible
I write, "A green dog loves decent purple dandelions"
That won't make sense to anyone without some drugs
I want to create something special
"A green dog loves decent purple dandelions"
What the hell does that mean?
They came from my fingers through my keyboard
My fingers were controlled by my mind
What was my mind thinking?
What was the imagery I was intending?
Christ, I wish I knew
He won't tell me what was in my mind
I don't think he would want to know
I just know one thing
With lines like that my mind is not with me
It left with a bottle of Kentucky whiskey
My mind is on vacation to a different planet
A planet in a galaxy so many light-years away
It may never come back to help me be creative
"A green dog loves decent purple dandelions"
That may be the last line I ever write
And THAT would be a hell of a way to be remembered

The Perfect House

There is the perfect house
Abandoned so long ago
Left to die all alone
Surrounded by the red desert
Scrub growing in place of grass
Kangaroos and cows die in the front yard
Geckos still run across the wasteland
Looking for a little shade
Water and food are kilometers way
A weekly trip just to survive
Still, that house is a piece of art
Telling a story that has to be told
Of someone trying a new life
Far away from the hassle of the city
Far away from a life that was not their own
There is the perfect house
Telling the history of a savage land
The problem is, no one will ever hear it
Before it is gone with the Outback winds
Buried under the blowing sands
And forgotten forever

History Lives

Let me go at five in the evening
Chasing the setting sun
Across the Great Dividing Range
Into the wild lands
Where stars are brighter
The skies are clearer
And the air smells sweeter
The aboriginal fires burn on the horizon
The moans of the didgeridoo fill the air
Even from so far away
History still lives
Let me travel west
Following my instincts
All the way to The Kimberley
A land, old when the Earth was young
Where time has never changed
Where history still lives

Little Sleeping Beauty

She lays there so nice and quiet
A princess without a crown
She dreams of flowers,
Candy, winged horses and dolls
She wears a pink dress, covered with flowers
Her red hair flows down across her shoulders
She smiles ever so slightly
A faint giggle comes from her closed mouth
She sounds so sweet as she stirs
Asking her mommy for water
So sweet
So innocent
Someday she will grow
She will marry
She will have a little princess of her own
Maybe she will dream of flowers,
Candy, winged horses and dolls
Wear a pink dress
Smile ever so sweetly
And ask for a glass of water
I am sure of one thing
She will be loved

Setting in the Western Ocean

The sun has watched me since dawn
It saw my anger
The depression that filled my mind
It saw the mistakes I made
And my fear of living
It gathered my pain within its fire
Carrying it across the sky
When the sun sets over the western ocean
It takes my problems along with it
The moon rises in the east
Bringing the coolness of the night with it

Allowing me to sleep
Taking me into a pleasurable world of dreams
Where my problems no longer exist
It is a place where I can live
Until the moon rests behind the western sea
And the day starts again

Your Own Reality
A tribute to artist Bobby Ross

Don't be stuck with reality
Find your own world
Make it the way you want
Color the sky violet
Make the grass blue
And the trees magenta
Place the birds under the seas
Let the whales fly among the clouds
And let the animals sing their own songs
Don't be stuck with reality
Do not let anyone tell you that you can't do it
It is your world
It is your reality
And because it is
It can never be wrong

Blessed Redhead

Let the fire fall from the skies
Let Heaven choose a few
To harness the light
A beauty unknown to man
A fiery mane of burning hair
Lit by the god's graces
With ivory skin
Covered with countless freckles
Each a fingerprint from Aphrodite

Only a few are blessed with such beauty
They have tempers to match their hair
Fiery yet controlled by passion
A rarity in this world
To be admired, treasured by man
Loved as no other should

Fill The Ute

Let's fill the Ute with ice
Stock it full of beer
Head into the bush
Have us a country party
Slim Dusty and James Blundell
Playing from my mate's CD
We want to get drunk
Finish off a case of XXXX
And not regret one drop
Don't anyone bring any Fosters
We won't drink it
We all want to cuddle
With a home grown country girl
One we have never met
But one we all know
Maybe we will even fall in love
Tonight there are no worries
No thoughts about tomorrow
Only tonight matters
The beer, the music and the girls
Nothing could make life better
So, let's fill the Ute will ice
Stock it full of beer
And enjoy living on this rock
Tonight, tomorrow will never come
As long as we are having fun

An Illusion Of Words

A girl, no way to know her age
Her looks are years younger than her age
Her mind smarter than her age
Her beauty is timeless among the ages
She sits and writes day after day
Places words in just the right place
She laughs at her ideas
She cries at how her writings play out
She is alone among a multitude of friends
Her thoughts jump between life and death
Love and hate, ar and peace
No one knows how her mind works
It is only a guess to say how she feels
She doesn't want anyone to know her
She is a ghost walking among the living
A spirit that can only be held in the mind
And that is how she will stay
Just an illusion of words

I Ask You Please

Please do not ignore me
It was not my fault I was born
I had nothing but love for you
I looked up to you
I needed you
And you just left me
I had no home
No food or water
No one to love
Against all odds I survived
I begged and stole
I slept in the narrowest of cracks
I was too young to do anything else
I looked and looked for you
Looked for anyone who would love me
I watch people walk by
They do not see me
They never even look

But, I am there in the shadows
Hungry, cold and all alone
Still, I survived and I asked one thing
Please do not ignore me

Long Distance Love

It is so very hard when you are so far away
It's only a couple of miles
Merely a stone's throw away
But it seems to be an insurmountable distance
We call, but it isn't the same
You are not beside me where you belong
My arms feel empty
My lips tremble wanting to feel your kiss once again
My heart aches when I think of you
It is so hard know that I am without you
Dreams of our love fill my sleep
My arms reach for you in the night
All they find is a cold emptiness
So my dreams and desires go unanswered
If only the miles would fade away
If I could look into your eyes and smile
I could see the feelings the miles hide away
And the distance would not matter any longer
I would be with you and nothing could be better
It is all I could ask
All I could ever want
But it is a dream that will never come true
The miles will never fade
My arms will be empty
But, in my mind, we will be together
Forever

A Tribute To Freddie Mercury

What happened?
Why did God take you away?
Your music soothed so many
Brought others to tears
Yet everyone danced and sang with you
Following your fingers on the piano keys
You cast your spell over thousands
Your voice was a gift from the gods
You took the stage you were blessed
And you blessed us with your songs
We didn't know that you were suffering, dying
You kept your pain a secret so we would not worry
You knew we would mourn before your life was over
You knew we would cry and not hear your last songs
How we miss you since you left
Your band continues on
Playing the music that you made famous
You made the music everything that it was
You changed music from the day you sang your first note
No one will ever give what you gave
You gave your life for your fans
We knew it and we loved you for it
Your goodbye left a void that will never be filled
Four words and just four words say what we feel
They are strong words that you gave meaning to
We hear them when we see you on a video
They echo through our ears as we hear your song
God Save the Queen and God bless Freddie
He will always be royalty in our hearts

Tribute To A Grocery Cart

I see it outside the store
Waiting for me
Calling to me
Offering to help my aching feet
Making it easier to walk the aisles
But, I know it is evil
It knows just how much money I have
Not a penny less or a penny more
It leads me past the cookies
Past the candy
And past all the things I shouldn't eat
Then it takes me to the register
Carrying all the junk I didn't need
To a girl with the sweetest smile
She knows its power
She counts up my items
Dollar by dollar she adds to the total
I know it is laughing at me
I know I have spent every last cent
Then it follows me to the car like an old friend
Helps me by waiting until I unload
Then it laughs again as I realize
That I had forgotten the milk I went in to buy
And it gets taken back into the store
To wait calmly for another victim
While I sit and curse that lonely grocery cart
The demon of the supermarket

The Cowboy Life

He spends so many days
Traveling the old cattle trails
From Oklahoma to Abilene
Day after day with no end in sight
Just other men, horses and cattle
Mile after mile
Storms and endless sun
Sand blowing across the plains
Tearing into his skin
Heat and rain
The cowboy waits for a single moment
To take time to relax and be himself
Away from the noise and the hardness
To lose his exhaustion
And just to take the time to look at his world
Sadly, that moment won't last for long
Tomorrow he'll be back on the trail
Surrounded by cowboys and cattle
And once again, despite the heat and the weather
He will love it
Because he knows one thing
It is his life and he will never give it up

The Normal Park Bench

It was just a normal park bench
Wood and metal
It was like so many others
Still, to him it was special
The most special place on Earth
It was where he met his only true love
Where they met every day for lunch
Where they shared their first of many kisses
Where he first said "I love you"
And where she agreed to be his wife
They took their children and grandkids there to play
And after years, they still went there for lunch

It was on that bench the she told him something
Something he didn't want to hear
His only true love was dying
And there was nothing they could do
For years he went to the bench for lunch
He talked to her as if she was still there
One day he left a flower at lunchtime
That bench never saw him again
And once again, it was a normal park bench
Wood and metal
It was just like so many others

Ned Kelly

A villain to some
A hero to most
He fought
He stole
And he killed
Stood up to the law
As he rode the outback
Robbing banks everywhere
Helping the people as he went
Stories would be told for years
Myths would become legend
The legend would become history
Ned Kelly, the man who fought and won
The man who died doing what only he could do
He is a part of Australiana
Part of the country that created him
Made him a villain
Made him a hero
Made him a legend

Drawing by Raeann McMillen

Through The Eyes Of A Child

Eyes of the deepest
They look at a world in a fresh way
Seeing snow and rainbows for the first time
She smiles in wonder at everything
Everything age has tarnished
She is so innocent and pure
Full of love and beauty
Everything we forgot as we grew
Should we take the time to look back?
Look at snow as nature's magic
Should we say awww when we see a rainbow

We could watch in amazement at a cloud
Imagining a bunny floating across the sky
Maybe we should look through her eyes
See what she sees
If only we could see it as a child does
Then the world would be a beautiful place

Dreamtime

Let me watch you sleep
Wrapped in an old quilt
Dreams fill your head
Showing you how your life should be
Making your every wish come true
Your lips show a faint smile
So soft that it could hardly be seen
Your eyelids flutter as if they are in a gentle breeze
Moved by invisible butterflies
A sigh fills the air
So tranquil and peaceful
What could you be seeing
I wish I knew what your nocturnal desires are
You may not know yourself
You may not remember what you saw
But somewhere in the world of the Dreamtime
You are happy

Ode To A Wave

Such beauty
Such ferocity
Such power
Traveling around the world
Pushed by tropical winds
You grow and fall
Only to grow ever stronger
Carrying ships and jetsam
Even moving lands before you
You are as destructive as you are beautiful
Yet, after your travels
At the end of your life
A child laughs and dances
As you tickle their feet as you roll across the sand
And then you are gone
Except in that child's smile

Did I Eat Dinner?

How could I have lost my mind?
I remember bits and pieces of my day
Eggs and pancakes for breakfast
Coffee and cream for lunch
What did I have for dinner?
Did I even eat dinner?
I sat across from a woman
I seem to remember that.
She talked and I answered
I think we talked
Did I hear anything or did I make it up?
Was she real?
Did I eat dinner?
I think I smelled a steak and baked potatoe
Or is it potato, I don't remember?
Could the smell have come from next door?
It could have.
They eat dinner every night
Or do they…I don't remember if I have neighbors
Did I eat dinner?
I don't remember
There is a plate in front of me
I don't remember how I got it
It has good smelling food
Pancakes, steak and home fries
Is this dinner?
Did I have dinner?
This is most likely breakfast
I think I missed my dinner
Did I have dinner?
I will never know
But I will eat my breakfast
And maybe later in the day I will have dinner
If I remember

The Wonder Of Youth

I was so young
Able to do anything
Willing to do everything
I climbed sandstone cliffs
I swam in rapids beneath a waterfall
Stayed up for days at a time
I drank more than I should have
Fought more fights that I wanted to
I walked until I didn't know my way home
I hung with people who I knew were no good
I even used drugs that weren't exactly good for me
I grew older
Some say a wee bit wiser
Memories take me back to my youth
Showing me things I will never do again
As my life nears its inevitable end
I wonder how I could have been so stupid

How many times did I almost die from my actions?
I placed my life in the hands of the fates
They led me to where I am now
But they allowed me to share the wonder of youth
And I would do it all again
If I could

The Kiss

A lifetime ago a young girl asked for a kiss
A kiss that was never given.
Her heart was full of a love she could never share.
Her voice spoke of her love many times.
But it did not fall on deaf ears
The young man's heart felt the same love
He was not allowed to say what his heart was telling him.
He just looked into her eyes and dreamt of a single kiss.
Their love faded as the moments went by.
In his dreams he lived that one day over and over again.
He hears her asking for a kiss.
He sees her eyes tear as he did not respond.
His heart dies a bit every day.
He sees himself taking her hand into his.
His lips touch her as softly as a butterfly wing.
And he wonders how his life would have changed
If he had granted a young girl's wish and,
Even for a single moment, he had shared his love with her

The Violinist

He sits on the corner of a building
Four stories above the world below
Playing his violin day after day
No one knows his name
They just know that there is beautiful music
They imagine that is coming from Heaven
Does it matter to this lonely man?
He doesn't care for fame or money
God has graced him with the gift of music
He could be a star
He could perform with a huge orchestra
He would rather play alone above the people
He plays just to make people happy
He loves it when people dance down the street
That man
That lonely man is an artiste
Too bad no one knows who he is
But that would not make him happy

Winter Hope

Winter winds blow
Grey clouds move in from the north
Waves of snow hide the colors of the world
People huddle quietly together, trying to get warm
Small beams of sun, heat the air for the merest of moments
Birds are silent
Animals scurry for cover
Gnawing on the nut they hid away

When the world was warm
Children play
Eating the snowflakes before they land
Sliding on water frozen to the ground
Throwing snow at their parents
Their laughter can be heard
Covering the sound of the howling winds
The only sounds of life to be heard
Trees stand strong
Leaves long buried
At the end of a branch a single bud
Giving hope that the cold will soon end
Hope of a newly found warmth
New life
New hope
All in the single bud of one single tree

I Have Never Told Anyone This

I lie next to you every night
The moonlight shining across your face
I listen to the stories you tell stories
Sharing those moments of your life
Embarrassments and triumphs
Tales of your first love
Those few that ended with making you cry
Those that ended in friendship
I listen to your hopes and dreams
Wishes you had as a little girl
Desires that flame your soul now
Plans for your future
You tell me of the one that you love
Little and cuddly it plays with you when I am not there
For hours I hear all about you
I do not just listen
I hear every word
I wonder how many others have you share this with
How many have been in the place I am?
Then you say the magic words I hoped to hear
"I have never told anyone this"
And I know that I am special.

My Name Is Love

My name is Love
I am the name everyone wants to hear
You pray your whole life just to hear it once
It is a name that can comfort
Bring two people together
Making their lives better, happier
It's also a name that can frighten
Ruin a relationship if it is used too early
Destroy hope if it is used too late
Four letters, one syllable, one word
That brought down the walls of Troy
Made Romeo and Juliet legends
Empires were built and destroyed because of me

Two lovers started a new life by just saying my name
My name is Love
Use my name sparingly
Only with an open heart
Only when it is spoken in truth
Will it be the one name spoken
That will heal a broken heart
Bring a smile to a young girls face
Give hope to an innocent child
And keep the world turning as it always should

Just Give Me An Idea

Just give me an idea
One thought to mull over
Something to challenge me
And make me wonder
Just give me an idea
One that will start a discussion
Something to spark a debate
And make me think
Just give me an idea
One that allows me to see differently
Something that changes my world
And lets me live life
Just give me an idea

About The Poet

Poet R.e. Taylor has been writing stories and poetry since the age of five years old. He has learned to see the words hidden inside of everything. He may see a stone, a picture or he may hear a song or even a sound on the street that makes him think of a story or poem. In the pages of *The Poetry of Everything,* he shows how much can be seen in the world, or in dreams without even looking.

Check out our other books at www.shadowlightbooks.com

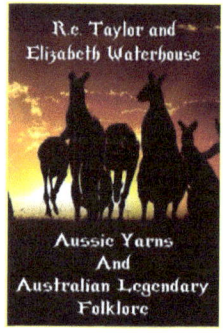
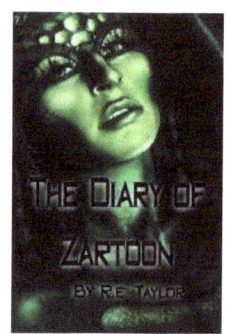
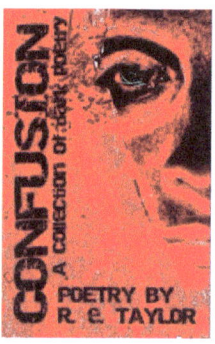

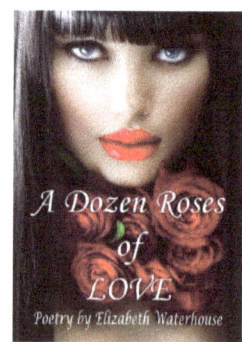

www.ingramcontent.com/pod-product-compliance
Lightning Source LLC
Chambersburg PA
CBHW040311050426
42449CB00019B/3482